VISION BOARD CLIP ART BOOK FOR BLACK BOYS

Kalishia Winston

YOUR FREE GIFT

As a way of saying thanks for your purchase, I'm offering the eBook *Teach Your Kids to Create Their Future with a Vision Board* for FREE.

To get instant access just go to:

KIDS.KALISHIAWINSTON.COM

FAMILY

I ♥ my family

GRANDMOTHER SON AUNT MOTHER SON
NIECE SON NEPHEW
BROTHER SISTER DAUGHTER
GRANDFATHER BROTHER AUNT BROTHER
COUSIN
MOTHER HAPPY FATHER
COUSIN DAUGHTER
UNCLE FAMILY NEPHEW
NEPHEW
SON NIECE GRANDFATHER AUNT
FATHER SISTER UNCLE
GRANDMOTHER
DAUGHTER MOTHER COUSIN BROTHER

FAMILY

NEW CAT

NEW PET

I choose to
think positive
about myself and
my future

All I need
to do is
take one step
at a time

I may stumble
and I may fall
but I will always
get up and
try again

I'm committed
to doing whatever
is necessary
to achieve my
goals

It's okay
to ask others
for help
when I need it.

CHALLENGES
help me
learn and
grow.

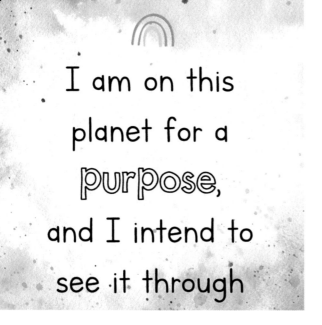

I am on this planet for a **purpose**, and I intend to see it through

Each day is a new **opportunity** to achieve my dreams

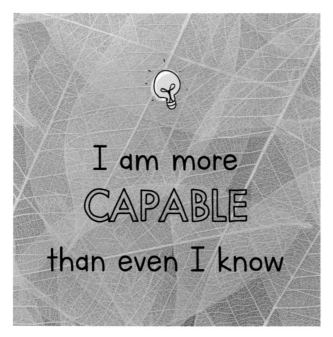

I am more CAPABLE than even I know

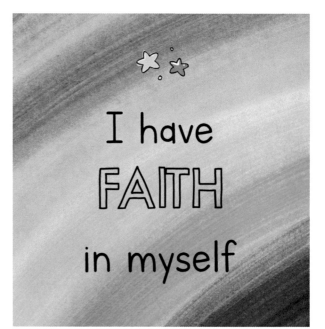

I have FAITH in myself

Being BRAVE means *taking a chance*

I approach new situations with an OPEN MIND

ask questions	help others	be fair
be kind	be positive	dream big
be grateful	I am enough	I am strong
I am talented	I am brave	I am smart
I want to see	I want to try	I want to learn
things I love	my goals	my plans
I want to achieve	happy	make new friends
never give up	love	hobbies
I will start	I will learn	keep trying
have fun	adventures	be me
be a star	school	every day

Made in United States
Orlando, FL
30 July 2024

49755738R00022